COMMON SENSE
IN SOCIETY

COMMON SENSE IN SOCIETY

DULCINEIA GOMES

Library of Congress Control Number: 2020913833
ISBN: Hardcover   978-1-6641-2092-1
                 Softcover   978-1-6641-2091-4
                 eBook   978-1-6641-2090-7

Scripture quotations marked KJV are from the Holy Bible, King James Version (Authorized Version). First published in 1611. Quoted from the KJV Classic Reference Bible, Copyright © 1983 by The Zondervan Corporation.

Any people depicted in stock imagery provided by Getty Images are models, and such images are being used for illustrative purposes only.
Certain stock imagery © Getty Images.

Print information available on the last page.

Rev. date: 01/18/2021

To order additional copies of this book, contact:
Xlibris
844-714-8691
www.Xlibris.com
Orders@Xlibris.com
815948

Introduction

There is not much common sense to the naked eyes on what the bible means. The word of God is understood when you are being guided by the holy spirit. Without it, is like reading just a book.

That is why it is important to pray before you begin to read the Word of God. The word of God is powerful that you need the holy spirit to understand it. I mean understand it in your heart, rather than just through the words. The holy spirit is like a protection or gatekeeper (figure of speech) which means, that you can read the Bible one hundred timed and not understand a single thing if your heart is not in it. Although there have been many credible scholars or prophets in history, there has also been many that were misled into misreading and misrepresented the word of God. So although we all need guidance in the beginning of our walk with God, we got to let go and be on the journey with God alone. That is why it is called a relationship with God. Just as a baby is nurtured to adulthood, we all begin as babies in the walk with God. And even as we get old, the learning does not stop. So this book is to give an insight on the daily struggles that Christians face in their walk-in society. It shows the difference between common sense, from a Christians perspective and worldly people. (The second part of the book talks about the biblical perspective.)

God gave us common sense, courtesy and respect Use it!
(Unknown)

It is with embarrassment to be living in this era with this generation. The 21 century has got to be the century with the most fucking idiots alive. Everyone wants to be with the next trend. They know everything about technology but the slightest clue about life. They rather not offend anyone instead of standing up for someone being abused. They rather praise an offender but condemn some for mistreating an animal. When did animals become more important than its master? When did animals get more rights than minorities? I'm for animal rights but let's get rights for every human being before getting to the animal kingdom. It's like everyone is suddenly went numb.

Like they forget what their ancestors did so that they can have a mediocre life.

Racism is both macro and on a micro level. It is unseen to the ones with their eye's clothes. But it's clearly on the micro level, but everyone is worried about being polite that its quietly killing them. Killing them like diabetes and other illnesses do you our mental and psychological state. The stress Is slowly distracting them, from realizing that they are hurting. Failing to see and recognize your oppression, is detrimental.

We are fixated on the next smart phone, that we forgot.

They forgot their ancestors getting attacked with water hoses, or just the thought of being locked in cages and set on fire.

Or working in farms and plantations for little or no pay.

Or those who risked their lives to come to the land of the great, just so their future off springs can have better lives.

All the civil protests and war that were fought. Those who left their homes and families to come to America. Should we not have more respect for their sacrifices? We are not worthy to enjoy or reap from what those that came before us did. We are existing rather than making a mark.

I'm speaking about every race. We don't know what to do or to be because we are so desensitized. We have been thought to be a selfish and individualistic society.

But we can only be so much as individuals. As individuals we will fall or cave. The more individualistic we become, the easier it is for us to come for each other. The more technology we come up with, doesn't always mean good. Many today are profiting off scamming millions across the world. And technology is making it super easy for the scammers.

America is known for being great. Known as the best nation, to be successful. It's known for its best Doctors, lawyers, Universities and the place to have the best opportunities. So, knowing that, why are we punish for wanting the best? For demanding respect from others? Nothing good comes easy. So why is that fact that if you are a fighter, of your life and those you love, why does that make you a rebel? I mean it's not like success is handed to you. This nation is great because of fighters of the past. People who speak out when they see people doing wrong, it is because they too want to make America greater, but for everyone, not just the rich.

"Birds of a feather flock together" is a popular saying, it is taken out of context. We tend to notice the humor in the phrase but fail to notice the truth and relevance of it. We fail to take notice when we wonder why people change, why people turn on you and what causes them to change.

When you introduce humor to many things, it prevents many from seeing its importance. Example "a wealth person may be snobby to the poor." The wealthy person may not intend to come across as a snob, but because of the struggles and hard work through the years, it might have changed them. Now they associate with other wealthy people, because their thinking patterns may relate. So when I mention the phrase "Birds of a feather flock together" I am simply talking about the ways of thinking. You will find this in everyday life. Whether it be business, politics, medical or fashion industry. A person will think differently, until they have reached a certain level, where they can compete and relate to others on a higher level. Just because the America is known for being great. Known as the best nation, to be successful. It's known for its best Doctors, lawyers, Universities and the place to have the best opportunities. So, knowing that, why are we punish for wanting the best? For demanding respect from others? Nothing good comes easy. So why is that fact that if you are a fighter, of your life and those you love, why does that make you a rebel? I mean it's not like success is handed to you. This nation is great because of fighters of the past. People who speak out when they see people doing wrong, it is because they too want to make America greater, but for everyone, not just the rich. If level of thinking may be higher, does not mean it is better. For example, salesmen think in a conniving way. Although it may be a great tactic for the industry, but it focuses on how much money you can get out of people. Another example, politics. Politics always have people with new and different mindsets with fresh ideas. As these people get exposure to the world of politics, they become tainted by the majority. They ways of thinking becomes effected, where they are forced to compromise their beliefs. In concluding my point, we plan our lives from a young age. Based on our environment and nature, our plans will more likely not fall through. Of Course there is God's plan, which will always triumph no matter how much we mess our lives up. Again we, as a society, tend to center our thinking process, based on who or what we associate ourselves with. Therefore not being able to put fort any change.

America is full of white privileged self-entitled people in it, which makes it impossible for things to change. White people swear that they don't have white privilege. I'm not saying that all white people have or use white privilege to get ahead. What I'm saying is that, white people who are "nice" show the other side of themselves once they feel threatened, don't like you or feel like you have double crossed them. They will be your best friends, until you are not kissing or catering to them. I am Of course referring to the older generations. The younger generations are more educated in racial topics.

Once you are a threat to a person of the Caucasian race, they will go by any means to destroy you, even if it means breaking the law. I'm not saying every white person is like that, but the majority are more likely to use their white privilege. But will end up getting away with breaking the laws because they created them. Meanwhile minorities are dealing with pettiness crimes and getting life sentences.

This is not by any means being racist, if you are stating the truth.

When is the Caucasian race going to realize that they still have advantages all over the world that other races only wish to have. Wishes like having the same advantage when it comes to employment, politics and the media, because of their race. A minority can be superior in a specific subject or skill, but because of the color of their skin, they are not allowed to get ahead or forced to dim their light.

Why does the Caucasian race have white privilege till this day? It goes back to slavery, when the black race was entirely under the control of the slave masters. After the civil rights movements, the murder of Dr. King and president Kennedy, it seems as if the will to fight died with them. There are some civil rights leaders today, but none can compare to Dr. king. It's like a sleep has come over these current generations living today. Although many protests are done, it rarely ends in progress. Lives are lost. It seems like the minority races lose a little more hope every single time someone is murdered for being a minority. It's almost as if our societies in America are falling into a big depression. Not only speaking on an economic level, but literally in a depression state. Although we may believe God, religion has always been a weapon used on the black race, in order to humble them. Therefore cause a Stockholm syndrome on the black race. I believe many are aware of it but know the repercussions of speaking on it.

The black community has taken so much loss in the last few decades, that has kept them under this Stockholm syndrome or trans.

I absolutely believe in forgiveness, but after forgiveness comes actions.

You can forgive people and still look out for yourselves. The problem is many are getting dumbed down with social media, having people believing that their voice will be heard. When in fact, it's an illusion. We have the illusion that our voices will be heard, meanwhile behind the scenes people are being targeted, persecuted. Not only by authority, but by strangers, cults, and other groups or subcultures. Instead of Americans standing together, they will hate on others, because they either know or think that they will get away with the crime.

Instead of standing together with their communities' partners and neighbors to fight for their rights as Americans, people rather be boneheads. People not helping the less fortunate because they have their noses up their behinds, because them are better off economically. If we all have to work, then we are equal. You've got to answer to a boss like the rest. Unless you own your own business. It doesn't take much to help others, but if you have no heart, then it's going to be extremely difficult.

However, there are many people of the Caucasian race that are not racist. It's the systematic racism that causes division between all races. I do feel that some white people are fighting a guilty conscience, that their ancestors caused. Some feel guilty to a point that they are afraid to say or do things in front of black people. These are the type of white people to defend the black race because of guilt. It's like having affirmative action outside the workplace. They are defensive because of the guilt more than because it's the right thing to do.

That is why there is no reason for racism to still exist. Even if they are doing the right thing because of their guilt, at-least they try.

Then there is the racism clueless white person. This type was more likely raised a very privileged life. It's not their fault that they are ignorant about racism. They may have lived a closed life and were under much surveillance by their parents.

If The black race were giving opportunities from the beginning of the end of slavery, they would be able to raise their children in a more advanced opportunity life. Because this did not happen, it has brought generational curses in black communities. There are some successful black folks today, but it does not compare to the Caucasian race. There is no equilibrium between the two. The white race is superior when it comes to wealth. Although the black race is superior in entertainment and sports, there is still an unbalanced system.

See when the systems have not changed much since slavery, how would you expect to change our communities. The system was built for the thrive of the white race. Even though physical slavery ended they still kept the same system.

If we ask for the white man to make some provisions to suit the black man, the white man will say that if he does, he will be breaking the law, or it would be unconstitutional. The last time I checked the blacks were on the frontline, with the Caucasian and natives to help fight foreign enemies off together. Therefore all deserve every benefit and rights of the constitution.

We need to respect our Americans just as much as the laws and constitution. After all America triumph because of the union of the races.

Being a minority in America can be like having all the money you want, but you cannot use it to buy much things. For someone born an American citizen, already has the rights to everything that America has to offer, but their skin color may pose issues.

We all want to get passed the slavery talk, but at least acknowledge it happened. White people cannot continue to act like black people are the problem because they keep bringing the topic of slavery up. The reason it is always brought up is because racism still exists today. The issue is like having an uncomfortable situation in a relationship, but not addressing it. Which then leads to more issues. Racism id passed through generations. We are not born racist.

Ignoring a problem will not make it disappear. The topic of slavery is like a giant elephant in a room, you know it's there, but no one will speak on it.

Another type of white people would be those who reside in the lower /poor parts of societies. These white people are not racist and are able to understand that race is not an issue there. They know that it has everything to do with class. By them going through some of the same struggles, help them get a better understanding of the racism problem blacks face today in America.

"Birds of a feather flock together" is a popular saying, it is taken out of context. We tend to notice the humor in the phrase but fail to notice the truth and relevance of it. We fail to take notice when we wonder why people change, why people turn on you and what causes them to change.

When you introduce humor to many things, it prevents many from seeing its importance. Example "a wealth person may be snobby to the poor." The wealthy person may not intend to come across as a snob, but because of the struggles and hard work through the years, it might have changed them. Now they associate with other wealthy people, because their thinking patterns may relate. So when I mention the phrase "Birds of a feather flock together" I am simply talking about the ways of thinking. You will find this in everyday life. Whether it be business, politics, medical or fashion industry. A person will think differently, until they have reached a certain level, where they can compete and relate to others on a higher level. Just because their level of thinking may be higher, does not mean it is better. For example, salesmen think in a conniving way. Although it may be a great tactic for the industry, but it focuses on how much money you can get out of people. Another example, politics. Politics always have people with new and different mindsets with fresh ideas. As these people get exposure to the world of politics, they become tainted by the majority. They ways of thinking becomes effected, where they are forced to compromise their beliefs. In concluding my point, we plan our lives from a young age. Based on our environment and nature, our plans will more likely not fall through. Of Course there is God's plan, which will always triumph no matter how much we mess our lives up. Again we, as a society, tend to center our thinking process, based on who or what we associate ourselves with. Therefore not being able to put fort any change.

People want to get on other's case when they are trying to stand up for a good cause. They are the same type of people to not have the guts to do the right thing but are right up-front row when it comes to the wrong things.

It is so easy to do the wrong thing. Doing the right thing is what it really means to be strong. Doing the right thing dhows your emotional intelligence.

We live in a backwards society. Good things are considered bad. The bad things are the new good.

Some people have to think about doing good. They have to literally meditate on it. And others are just good natured. Everything they do, is for the good of others and the environment.

Then there are those people who won't do bad things, but they have no problem being used to do bad things.

They call it being a good citizen.

Yes that is the delusion of many, being a good citizen.

Student Loans

When it comes to student loans, many have mixed feelings about the topic. I am one of those people. I have student loan debt, which will be one of the reasons why I may never own a home. The thing about the situation that I don't understand, is how are people supposed to pay them back, if they cannot get employment How can I get experience in a job if you don't ever get an opportunity? Banks will give loans to college students, but will deny most loans for small businesses? It doesn't make sense. If I'm starting a business, it means that I will be able to pay it back.

If I'm taking a student loan, it's not a sure thing that I am going to get employed. Not that I don't want to but because the economy is going downhill.

People live to die, rather them dying to live. For example, why do we care so much about where or how we are buried after death? God only cares about the soul after the body is dead. If I'm dead, why would I care? See the way they get everyone, is by putting the guilt of leaving a bill for their family. But society doesn't mind kicking their children out of their homes once they are of legal age. They just want to be part of everything and everyone, they don't bother thinking for themselves. They will just ho along rather than being a leader.

My thing is that nobody is concerned about getting to a solution. They are so focused and concerned about the problem. It's like instead of wanting to make it right, instead its "oh they found out our mistakes, let's get them"

Everyone is running on their own egos instead of as a group, that's why we will always stumble and fall.

How is it that some people can think clearly, and others are blind or choose to be blind? How do we function as a society when we all have our own accords?

If you are gay, but you get upset at others for calling you gay, what does that say about you? If you cannot accept yourself, why should I? Are you mad for staying in the closet or at others for pushing you out? When you are confident and comfortable in your skin, you will not care what others think, even if I don't agree with you. We both have that right to disagree.

You as a person, cannot tell me to put such and such away in order for me to be blessed by you. Only God has the right to tell you to put old things away so he may bless you. An employer does not have the right to tell his employees that they will promote them, if they quit their second job. A "friend" doesn't have the right to tell you to break up with your other friends. A university does not have the right to keep your degree from you if you are also attending a second school. My point is, if you are or want to bless someone with something, do it because they deserve it, not because they are not making you happy or not doing what you want them to do.

We live in a petty world, where any littlest speck, can be reason why someone treat good or the opposite. God is not prejudice about his blessings, why should we as humans be. People who are problematic are always looking for problems. Not to solve them, but to relish in the drama and to see what they can take from others. They need a line of supply. I mean, many are like vampires, are only in others' lives as a parasite. For example, a dude with a few baby mommas, will come in your life to cause more problems. In the meantime, trying to make you look like you are the problem when you were living your life. You might have one child, but this person makes you out to look like some whore. Really? When he's the one with two or three baby mommas? I'm not saying that all baby mommas are problematic. I am a single mother. And I'm always going to stick up for other sisters, of course if they are in their right mind, because I know the struggles that single mothers face every day. The struggles they face because of society marginalizing them. Because instead of men realize that women, especially single mothers are treated poorly in society. Without women, society wall cave. Many programs that is "supposed" created for women are nothing more than society's Affirmative action. We don't want to be labeled as a sexist society, so therefore we will create just enough, to keep women in their place. We will not create more than enough programs, to ensure that women get the equal opportunities that men do.

Society wants to use God's commands to remind us of our places. But do you remember what commands that God has for you? As a society, as a leader, as a man? Before people tell others where they belong, tell them to clean the specks on their eyes first.

Because we as a society, no longer live according to biblical terms and no longer following God's commandments, men and women are left to figure things out. You figure out what works for themselves, rather than for each other. This is so, because the level of divorce and single parent homes are skyrocketing high. Never been married men and women separate after having children. The mother is more likely to have custody of the child. In society and family members eyes, its best for the child to live with the mother. But they don't see the harm it does to the children and the mother. Not to say that some single fathers do not struggle, but this topic speaking on single motherhood, because it is biblical for a woman to raise her children. However, God also says that the father should be in the children's lives, more than what society expects or requires.

Just because statistics show that there are more non-custodial fathers paying child support, than there are non-custodial mothers paying child support, doesn't mean that things are all good. Single fathers paying child support are more likely to spend less time with the children, because they either choose to, the other parent is preventing them from seeing the children, or they feel like paying support is doing their part as a parent. Which is incorrect. Fathers who pay for child support, are paying to help support the child in financial ways. In no way does paying child support make you father of the year. The same for the single mother. You need to spend time and teach your child. Then this just causes friction and a whole bunch of unnecessary stress on the family.

Another strain that single parent homes have, is that all the burdens of raising children is put on that one custodial single parent. It's very tough to raise a child on your own, especially if the other parent only chooses to be buddies and have fun with the children, showing and teaching them nothing. Children with no discipline can be extremely difficult to handle.

The next strain I want to talk about is working for single mothers.

Most of us know that children who have At least on parent at home, tend to be stronger and more confident as adults.

But today's society encourages single parenthood. Particularly the single motherhood. Although society encourages this behavior, society does not provide the effective solutions to cope or handle single motherhood. Your telling me that I should be a super woman, that I can work and raise children in a single home? But jobs in society does not pay well enough to support children and relieve stress from my home? Society forces the noncustodial parent to pay child support but doesn't force them to spend time with their children. The way the states forces noncustodial parents to pay child support, is by penalizing them with the removal of something, most cases it's the driving license.

While society is busy encouraging single parents to pay child support, the custodial parent is left in a place where they are made to look like, just takers. Why doesn't the state obligate the noncustodial parent to make it less difficult for the custodial parent, who is usually trying you work. But they cannot work due to the children. child support is for the child. The single parents still have lives that they would like you live. Many noncustodial fathers contribute less than half of their times to raising their children but expect full time progress. They fail to see that the child is half their genes. Some fathers parent their children like they are helping or babysitting.

I don't mean to bash single fathers. Making my point, single custodial mothers have less chance to live a stress less life, and more difficult in living according to the standards of the bible. Society is an anchor for single mothers, but when your anchored for a long time, you cannot improve your quality of life.

Society preaches girl power and feminism but kick single mothers down for not being able to make it out. The reason I decided to address Dingle mother's id because men are built differently. There are always labor ready jobs for men. But do you expect mothers to get their hands dirty and still be able to walk with her head up high with class. If she's got to bring out her masculine energy to work, then turn on her femininity when she's headed home? Why would society encourage this behavior? For a woman to be the man and woman at the same time? Not mentioned when she gets home too tired to spend time with her child. Everyone is always ready to call out the single mothers with custody of their child, like they just want to be dependent on everyone. There may be some who take advantage of the system and the non-custodial parent, but not all custodial single parents are alike.

You just get tired of hearing the same incorrect comments about many dingle mothers.

I'm going to break down some situations to better help others understand where I'm coming from.

Many say that non-custodial parents (in this case fathers) pay and pay child support till they are dry. But They don't mention the missed payments. By the time they catch up with the payments, they've dug themselves in a whole. A lot of times we may get screwed by the system, but the state has no reason to lie about unpaid child support.

Many run from their responsibilities as a parent, but little do they know, that its less expensive to raise your own child. When you pay child support to the custodial parent, you are basically paying them to raise your child. (speaking for some mothers)I have to do my part as a mother (and also do your part as a father. ("On occasions I can have a break when you decide to take the children for Two days.")

I just believe that some noncustodial parents would've feel like they have to put a price tag on their child. A mother will always do so much more than expected, therefore you should not base the upbringing of your children as if it is an annoying chore, that must be done.

"This "state blaming" excuse has to stop. You are only doing transactions between you and the state." The state does not stop you from seeing your children, unless the custodial parents file motions and restraining orders. That is a separate issue. But I just thought I would elaborate on the issues burdening single parent homes, especially single mother homes.

Looking crazy can be a blessing. When you've been putting God on every part of your life, its common to lose a little touch with society. Especially if you've been staying away from society. The process of "crazy" is the mind being over worked. After you get through that crashing phase, you start healing.

What society calls "in the middle of craziness" that's when God speaks to you. Just like He speaks to us through our dreams, near death experiences and in the most unusual ways. God speaks to us when we are at the point of no control. He cannot speak to us if we are controlling our lives. We must submit ourselves to God. Submission is the way most relationships work here on earth. People on earth choose who they want to submit to. But to have a reason relationship with God, your only choice is to submit yourselves to God. Understand that God does not speak the language of arrogance or pride. Those two come from the enemy. Good and evil cannot coexist when it comes to God. That is the reason he is separated from us in heaven. Not because he wants to be separated from us. What father wants to be separated from His children. Because we are all born sinners, we must repent of out wicked ways if we want to be in heaven dome day.

But if we are, he on earth, we will continue to be sinners.

But we should not call or label people crazy, simply because we do not understand them.

The Jews and romans thought Christ as being crazy before they crucified Him on the cross.

Jesus was crucified for calling himself king of kings. Which was thought of as blasphemy against God.

Seriously. What do they do when you stand up for your beliefs? Institutionalize you.

If you are outspoken, you are made to look unstable.

When you defend your children, that came from you, they see you as a threat.

Can you do anything that you don't have to walk on eggshells in society?

Like for example, the lgbtq community. We are all being divided as people. Why does everyone else who does not identify with the lgbt community, have to be punished, for wanting to retain our values.

If it weren't for society wanting to know every crumb about you, so they can have their labels, we would not have hatred amongst us.

The lgbtq community are made to believe that they are hated by many and by God. On the other side Christians and others are also being

Fed lies that the lgbt is out to hate, and we therefore we should hate back. It is all political. Just like the media can destroy a politician's reputation. That's the way the game goes.

The devil is the biggest gangster there has ever been. We don't give him much credit either.

Which just shows that many of us suck as spiritual beings. We walk around like, I know this, I have that, like we have reached the topic of mount olive.

Did you know that politics is driven by those who exercise control, power and Arrogance? Seriously, I'm speaking from a spiritual viewpoint.

Anyways, control, power and arrogance are some key point that the enemy uses in order to enslave and keep many in bondage.

I'm not saying everything about politics is evil, but they like to separate from Godly things. It just makes you think. Are they trying to cater to only one group of people?

If you are for all, then let all be involved. I understand some people are natural born leaders and that is why they are in leadership roles. But it's not becoming a leader that is the struggle. The key is to stay a leader and become a better leader. Just as God let you be put up there, he can take you down if you are not working for his purpose.

BIBLICAL PERSPECTIVE

What does it mean to have biblical names today? Back in the bible days you were named according to your characters and, what you did for work, and destiny. Some people let their name dictate who they will be in life. Others will live carelessly. That is why putting labels on people of societies is dangerous. Not only are people not able to live and hold up standards which their names hold, but some who become terrible people, can have a biblical meaningful name, that is totally the opposite of their character. Now you might say, "what's your point about silly names." Well I believe that there is power attached to words, especially biblical or divine related words. We should appreciate them and take them seriously, because they send messages to others relating to God, whether its false or true.

Back in the bible days, most people were righteous and then there were the unrighteous ones, like law breakers, heretics, and act. As the world became more "civilized ", whatever that means. We surely have evolved but still act uncivilized, like do not know better. If you think about it, we have become so distant from God, even though we have technology that makes our lives better. We are ungrateful. We now live in the worst times when it has to do with God. Even in history, during battles and wars, people stood for something. People stood up for God. Now today, we are standing up for ourselves. I am not saying that we should not look out for our well brings, but we forgot the most important, which is God. The more we evolve, the more we separate from God. It doesn't have to be this way, but we can have our cake and it too.

My point is that humanity has fallen even shorter of the glory of God. You can have a biblical name and be a serial killer. You can have an offensive name, and still be a child of God. Another point I am trying to make is that, just because someone is not an Israelite, does not mean that they will not prosper in life if they aren't continually following God's laws and be obedient. worship the Almighty God. It is more of who you worship verses who you are. When Christ died at the cross, he died for all, including the gentiles and every other sinner. He would be a hypocrite if he required us to love our neighbors, for him not to die for his neighbors. Christ taught not just by parables, but also thought by example. He lived by example. He was the perfect role model and a perfect example of what a parent should be. Even those who do not believe that Jesus is God in the flesh, still believe that he was the most perfect man to ever walk this earth.

See the devil has everyone focused on being right, that we forget to do what is right. Everyone wants things but are not willing to work for it. The only things they will work for is their carnal self. Everyone wants to be a teacher, but they do not want to acknowledge the great teacher. Many wants to build, but you do not know the Great architect. People believe that king Solomon was the greatest architect, but it was Christ. It was God who allowed Solomon to possess such wisdom, through the blessings from his fathers who came before him. We all know that although Solomon possessed this great wisdom, but he was a sinner, Fornicating and married women with other gods. Which shows that we all fall short of the glory of God. Just because we have a title attached to our names, but in the end we all need God's mercy and guidance. Like king David, who had God's protection and blessings, committed sin. He took a righteous man's life, and then took his wife. I am saying that just because you are in a platform, it does not make you perfect, you are still dinners that need that need the grace of God. Once again, even though your ancestors we righteous in the eyes of God, that does not excuse you from following the laws of God.

We follow the laws of the land. We follow regulations and rules at our jobs. Why don't most people follow the laws of God? Because probably do not know how important their souls are. We live the law of the land from the time we open our eyes in the mornings till we close our eyes at night. Even in school they are teaching the way you act in society. They are preparing you to know the ways of conduct in society. But church is just once a week, for 2 hours. By the time the church staff gets through the announcements, the worship, and tithing, people are looking at their watches before the pastor has not even begun to preach. I am going to exaggerate a little bit, but a lot of time is wasted on the church building and announcements. Then the pastors got to rush their way and cram everything in less than an hour. I would say ninety percent of church time is a big show, a facade. People go to church to hear Gods words. After hearing the Gospel, people should not be tired or bored. Ten percent is the pastor's preaching time. It takes up to five percent of that time the pastor is preaching you get into the word of God. That last five percent of the time everyone is getting antsy and the pastor is closing the sermon. So you leave church with a false high that is caused by getting into the word, with the excite that you get to go out to eat, like you have worked a double shift. I am not blaming the church goers; some are just sheep. We need to hold the pastors more responsible because church is getting to be a network rather than a house of the lord. The church is not a democracy, but you got a first family mentality in church that they are more concerned about appearances. That Just shows that even some pastors do not know Gods words or don't have the grace and sanctification of God. They lack faith in his words. God says to plant the seeds and He will nurture that seed. If you believe in his words in the first place, you will know that the pastor and his family always have a perfect look, but the church is falling apart. When I say church, I mean the people, the church goers. If everyone is leaving like they are tired, then then they did not grasp the message, because they were too busy sleeping. However, I hold church goers responsible for going to church at the last minute. We all have had that rush their ways to church.

Do not get me wrong, I am not saying all churches are in trouble. But why is the church trying to be like the world? Pastors need to step up and stop being so comfortable being lukewarm. . Many Pastors today are not sanctified. They see being a pastor a just having a job, especially the younger pastors today . Many are in management positions without the qualifications. Many or becoming pastors without the calling of God. Any follower of God can be a witness and share the gospel, but it takes God's qualifications for you to pastor. How will you know? The bible says to test their spirits. Going to bible college does not qualify you. God does not care about your degrees. You are dealing with souls, not a job just for a paycheck. The sanctification of God Should be your degree. This is what God means by, "You can't serve both God and mammon." It is a big responsibility to be a leader. You do not want to lead God's people astray, because there are great consequences. Just like leaders in communities, if they break the laws, they too must receive the consequences by the law. God says there is punishable consequences for leading His people to condemnation.

When people in communities struggle, are in danger, feel unsafe and etc., and are not able to get help, satisfaction or get awareness to others, they will develop a "Do what you got to" mentality, if they cannot get anyone to take them seriously. All of times things that happen in life, are difficult to either be proven to the Authorities, or it just sounds too crazy. It might sound more elusive, rather than more tangible. When it comes To God, it is similar. It is supernatural but to unbelievers, God is not supernatural. To have faith in the Lord, you must believe that God is willing and capable of all things.

People who go through things that are unbelievable and that is where you need to have faith. Having a relationship with God is a little strange and can seem crazy to others., Those that are in danger of many health issues, including mental health, which can then lead to them committing crimes. It may lead to other crazy things, that is not of the Lord if we are not careful. I am not in any way saying that it is ok to commit crimes while dealing with mental illness. I am simply saying that the state has a difficult time helping believes of Christ and spiritual beings, because of the separation of church and state. I believe that had the state not been separated from church, the state would be more willingly to help faith seekers. The state would be more informed to help, rather than be quick to labeling individuals. We understand that no two individuals are exactly alike, therefore we need freedom of religion.

Our communities and events that take place in communities, can cause people to withdraw from society. I mean mental withdrawal from society.

However, if you are forced into this state of mind, that is a different issue. What I mean is, when you gave perpetrators who intentionally cause you to withdraw from society, that is a bigger problem. It is a problem because, the people who are put there to help you, are the ones causing your distances. If someone going through this has spirituality and strong minded, this person has a good chance of recovery. See someone who does not believe in a higher power, the chances are slimmer. These types of people are more likely to get addicted to pills, alcohol, and other substances. They are more likely to hurt themselves or even resort to suicide. See for any person going through this ordeal, is already feeling alone, and non-trusting of everyone.

When you believe in a higher power, you are going to be alright, At least psychologically.

Let us say an atheist, is in this situation. If they do not believe in God, do not trust anyone, then what else is there left for them? I do not mean you sound harsh, but it true. If you cannot rely on family of friend, money and materialism is not going to help. They tried everything they can to get authorities to handle the issue, but nothing comes from that. Unless you use that as an excuse to do bad things. These bad things could potentially never be bad, in the eyes of the one who is on survival mode. My question is, how would an atheist handle the situation after contacting authorities, but had no success? Now if you do not believe in God, then nothing could deter them from doing anything. There is no God to keep these people in check. I am not incinerating that all atheist, are more likely to be reckless, but merely an assumption. (Which would explain why religion was a good thing for slave masters during slavery.) Religion is not completely bad but is often abused to manipulate and deceived people. Religion is a deterrent for crimes and deters people from heading to wrong paths in life. Although we have a merciful God, that is full of grace and willing to forgive your sins. With the laws of the land, it is a different story. God will forgive, but still discipline you. While the law of the land will punish you for your crime and keep a record of your crime. Jesus Christ forgives, and God forgets your sin. This is especially important to know about God because it effects the way you think. Once God forgives your sins, you get a fresh start. A person who gives their life to Christ, is considered a new creature. Meanwhile the laws of the land keep records and scores. If you are looking for employment, your records could go against you. In God you are a new person with a fresh start. I guess that is the whole point of separation of church and state. Although this separation is a disadvantage on Christians, the law needs to hold accounts for everyone else. That is one similarity that God's laws and the law of the land have in common. God is no respect of people. The us constitution also respects no Establishment or person. Meaning that Everyone is to be treated equally and cannot discriminate. So at times it may seem like things which have no morals, are being allowed into our legislation. Although we may believe that it is immoral, others have the right to choose what to do, of course if it does not infringe our rights granted by the constitution. Just as God gives us the choice to do good or evil, if we know what the consequences. Which leads to my next point.

SEPARATION OF CHURCH AND STATE

Malachi chapter 2 verse 17

"You have wearied the Lord with your words; Yet you say, in what way have we wearied him? In that you say. Everyone who does evil is good in the sight of the Lord, and He delights in them. Or where is the justice?"

Now we all know about the separation of church and state. Even thought at times it seems that the state issues spill over into the church. But that is another topic. What I wanted to talk about is, about how society reacts to tragedies and towards God when tragedy hits. Everyone knows how much societal tragedies impact our communities. We blame God for letting bad things happen to us, when we are the ones who reject him. We are a spoiled and self-righteous societies, that think that we can act in anyway, and still expect blessings from God. Although God gave us the free will to do as we please, it does not exempt us from consequences. We cannot act in whichever way that we feel is right and expect God to intervene when we want him to. We cannot take him out of public places and then hope or expect Him to be there. Its either one or the other. We punish our children for reading their bibles in school. Then when there are school shootings, we cannot get mad at God. We told him that He is not wanted there when we forbade his children from reading their bibles. People do not know that but having praying teachers and praying students in an education institution, is a blessing. Because of their prayers and just being children of God, means that God and his blessings is always with them.

Another point I want to make is, that

When God is not in your presence, then who do you think is? With the way things are going on in the world, many people, including children are being attacked spiritually. Once you shut God out of someone, it leaves a space for the enemy to fill. We are living in the times of spiritual warfare. Children also face attacks from the enemy every day. Now imagine how many children are in one school, just sharing all kinds influences.

Therefore we need to protect our children by telling them to keep up with their prayer lives. There are kids every day, who are going through something emotional or traumas, that need to be in our prayers.

Another example of the times we disrespect God, are during natural disasters.

We complain, why would God let these things happen to us, while we act like we can do it all without Him. As soon as something horrible happens, we get in the excuse's mode. We make every excuse while we do not spend time with God, instead of doing the opposite.

It is like we discipline our children when they are disobedient. But God forbade us to think that God always punishes and disciplines. Whether we like it or not, God is the creator. That would make us his children, do we cannot tell him how to do something that he created. God disciplines those he loves.

Separation of Church and State

Malachi chapter 2 verse 17 says

"You have wearied the Lord with your words; Yet you say, in what way have we wearied him? In that you say. Everyone who does evil is good in the sight of the Lord, and He delights in them. Or where is the justice?"

Now we all know about the separation of church and state. Even thought at times it seems that the state issues spill over into the church. But that is another topic. What I wanted to talk about is, about how society reacts to tragedies and towards God when tragedy hits. Everyone knows how much societal tragedies impact our communities. We blame God for letting bad things happen to us, when we are the ones who reject him. We are a spoiled and self-righteous societies, that think that we can act in anyway, and still expect blessings from God. Although God gave us the free will to do as we please, it does not exempt us from consequences. We cannot act in whichever way that we feel is right and expect God to intervene when we want him to. We cannot take him out of public places and then hope or expect Him to be there. Its either one or the other. We punish our children for reading their bibles in school. Then when there are school shootings, we cannot get mad at God. We told him that He is not wanted there when we forbade his children from reading their bibles and forbade them from praying in schools. People do not know it, but to have praying teachers and praying students in an education institution, is a blessing. Because of their prayers and just being children of God, means that God and his blessings is always with them.

Another point I want to make is, that

When God is not in your presence, then who do you think is? With the way things are going on in the world, many people, including children are being attacked spiritually. Once you shut God out of someone, it leaves a space for the enemy to fill. We are living in the times of spiritual warfare. Children also face attacks from the enemy every day. Now imagine how many children are in one school, just sharing all kinds influences.

Therefore we need to protect our children by telling them to keep up with their prayer lives. There are kids every day, who are going through something emotional or traumas, that need you be in our prayers.

Another sample of the times we disrespect God, are during natural disasters.

We complain, why would God let these things happen to us. God lets things happen or does things that we sometimes do not understand as humans. Especially worldly persons. We have got to have faith in Him before we go through struggles, because our faith will be challenged.

It is like we discipline our children when they are disobedient. But God forbade us to think that God always punishes and disciplines. Whether we like it or not, God is the creator. That would make us his children, do we cannot tell him how to do something that he created. God disciplines those he loves.

A spiritual person, who believes in God, whether his or her beliefs sounds insane, are at an advantage. Spiritual people already enjoy spending time alone. Being alone is not exactly lonely when you believe in God. (No disrespect to spirituality, but it is like a child with an imaginary friend.)

Most only child and unique personality having children, usually acquire an imaginary friend. Therefore, people who do not understand the power of God, is so quick to assume that a follower of Christ as a person with mental illness. This is one of my descriptions of what it is like to be a follower God.

We are look upon as weird and strange, but We are children in the site of God. That is What Christians should strive for, to have a pure heart as children, so that we may inherit the kingdom of God. He is our friend and confidante. Just like a child, telling his secrets to their imaginary friends. They appear as unique and odd children. Just as Christians appear as weirdos. Christians are weird because they gave faith in Christ, not the world. Christians are weird because, they have encountered things that this world does not offer. The world can only offer fleshly and worldly things. Meaning things that is seen by the naked eyes. The world cannot see your emotions and feelings. The world cannot see your traumas and fears.

For this specific reason, I believe that spiritual individuals are more mentality strong than individuals who have no belief system. Whether the world thinks that religion is a crock, or hindrance, your faith is the only one that will get you through tough times.

Sometimes the world can be envious of your relationship with God. They do not know why they do not like you. But they just do not. It is the light of God shining through you. That light in you will disturb the demons in some people. That why we must always have the armor of God on. The enemy is always searching for different routes to get to you. So he will send his servants, people who have not yet submitted to the living God. Therefore exposing themselves to be possessed by demonic spirits.

Some people like to live amid ignorance, and some are not even aware of their ignorance. I do not mean ignorance in the sense of academia but relating to lack of wisdom or common sense. People who go with the flow never questioning anything or anyone. But as soon as someone that is questioning things come along, they are the first ones to criticize you for doing what they wish they could do.

Wisdom that should come as a person ages, seems to be an epidemic. It almost seems as people are doing the opposite. It has always been seen ad hip to be or act young, but people have taken it to the extreme. It says in Proverbs chapter 9:10kjv "The fear of the lord is the beginning of wisdom, and the knowledge of holy is understanding."

Wisdom does not come to all.

With aging, especially if so, many people reject God and his ways. More importantly why we should submit to the God of heaven.

I just had to share it with everyone. Most people do not understand why we were put here on earth. Even those who say they are spiritual. We think our purpose was to help the economy boom, take vacations and buy things. Yes, we need some of those things to be able to do what our purpose is. But not a-lot of us achieve it or will not achieve it.

We were created for the purpose of the highest. We were created for his glory, not the other way around. So when tragedy happens, it is not only affecting us. It affects God because he loves us. Like any parent who disciplines their child for bad behavior, God does the same with his children. God wants to reward and bless us, be he cannot if people continue to be disobedient.

When we lose material things or struggle through life, we say What kind of God would let tragedy happen? Again, we put value in things that are not. He wants us to understand that things of this world are not everlasting. That is why he does things in his own way. We are children to God, no matter how old we are. Would you let a child make an adult decision? That is why we have laws on land protecting children. Why is it that men just want to be the discipliner but not submitter? How are our children supposed to listen and obey adults and authority, if we cannot submit to the authority of God?

The bottom line is that we do not really know God, because we do not know him. We do not make time for him.

Which is why God lets the enemy touch your life. The absent of Good is Evil. It is one or the other. It is your choice. Just like you respect your boss and business owners to build a connection, why not build a connection with God. After all you do want blessing from God. Since I have struggled much of my life, I realized that God is a God of doing, not just saying. Unfortunately as humans we do not always learn obedience. Sometimes God must let tragedy hit our lives, so we can appreciate him. We gave to lose to appreciate others. We got to go through testing periods in our lives, to be able to learn how to trust him. Although many of us do not know who God is, He however does. God knows everything about a person. God can number the hair in on your head. He is that great that He can number every single speck of rocks that make up sand on the beaches of every corner of the earth.

People these days are reliable among themselves. They feel like they do not need a divine guidance because they have their lives under control. But did you know that the devil never bothers the ones that he knows he is got? Meaning that if you do not have God in your life, then he is got you. What is the opposition of good? Bad. So if God is good, and you do not have him in your life, then you have the opposite. What many do not know is that anything that is not holy, is antichrist. It must be compared to the biblical word, not the worlds views of good and bad.

THE SPIRIT OF IGNORANCE

Some people like to live during ignorance, and some are not even aware of their ignorance. I do not mean ignorance in the sense of academic but relating to lack of wisdom or common sense. People who go with the flow never questioning anything or anyone. But as soon as someone that is questioning things come along, they are the first ones to criticize you for doing what they wish they could do.

Wisdom that should come as a person ages, seems to be an epidemic. It almost seems as people are doing the opposite. It has always been seen ad hip to be or act young, but people have taken it to the extreme. It says in
Proverbs chapter 9:10kjv "The fear of the lord is the beginning of wisdom, and the knowledge of holy is understanding."

Wisdom does not always come.
With aging, especially if so, many people reject God and his ways.

People these days are reliable among themselves. They feel like they do not need a divine guidance because they have their lives under control. But did you know that the devil never bothers the ones that he knows he is got? Meaning that if you do not have God in your life, then he is got you. What is the opposition of good? Bad. So if God is good, and you do not have him in your life, then you have the opposite. What many do not know is that anything that is not holy, is antichrist. It has you be compared to the biblical word, not the worlds views of good and bad.

I am not saying that a person will remain ignorant if the refuse to accept God, but it is the most satisfying. It is free. Fearing the lord will humble you, and make you realize that the wisdom you will receive from God, is everlasting. It can be passed down for generations. Meanwhile the knowledge I obtain from man., is not absolute that it will be used every day of your life. The know of God is thirst quenching. You will never thirst again with His knowledge.

I am not saying that a person will remain ignorant if the refuse to accept God, but it is the most satisfying. It is free. Fearing the lord will humble you, and make you realize that the wisdom you will receive from God, is everlasting. It can be passed down for generations. Meanwhile the knowledge I obtain from man., is not absolute that it will be used every day of your life. The know of God is thirst quenching. You will never thirst again with His knowledge.

A lot of men and women of God are misled or confused about the expectations of God. They think that they got to put a show for the church and the world. When they are both are walking around with heavy hearts and not feeling fulfilled in life. Even with a marriage and family, it is possible to feel emptiness inside. That is because only God can fill that void that you try to fill. When a man and a woman are walking in according to God's ways. One person can do so much with God on his or her side, but a married couple in God, can achieve so much more. Together they can change generations.

Real men n real women of God Build communities and help build nations.

The thing with non-God-fearing people, is that you automatically think, it is because of your sins that you struggle, meanwhile when something happens to them, they want to get the whole society involved. They try to change other ways of living, just to make it convenient for them. Meanwhile in the process making it inconvenient for everyone else.

But the devil loves sin, so he is going to let it happen. That is why he does not care if the world is in bondage and condemned. God sent his son to the world, so that everyone who believes in him shall not perish but be saved.

I believe one of the reasons why people do not believe or like God, is because they do not know who he is. And you will not know him if you do not believe he exists. It takes a little faith before faith. What I mean is, you need to take that leap, give God a chance for him to prove that he is real. A relationship with God will not just boom after the first encounter with God. It takes discipline and consistency. You got to work at your relationship with God just as you do with people, If not even more. A relationship with God is the most important relationship you can ever have. I am not saying to stop doing your things like hustling and keep yourself groomed. It is just boneheaded people who try to prove a point or test God by making your life difficult. They want to see if they can get God to react. Like God ever needs to prove himself to us when we feel like it. Some people confuse power and strength with control. Just because you can, do not mean it should be done. It takes more power and self-control to hold back. Not holding yourself from controlling others only says your strength only goes as far as yours power or materials gains will allow you too. This is the main reason child have great imaginations. They only know what Godly given information, till we kill that innocence. Many people fail to see that God is supernatural. Therefore, creating television shows, movies and books that destroy the idea about God's capabilities before it is discovered. That is the exact thing that the devil did before Christ. He discredited him, so that when he arrived, people would not be expecting or believe in him. By creating Religion, people lose sight of faith. You do not need religion to have faith. I believe that religion was created by the devil to separate and divide people.

That is why God says you need a relationship with him to be saved, not Religion to be saved. Religion works for society. It helps keep order and can to a point discipline people, but that is the furthest that you as an individual will get. To obtain a high level of spirituality, you must take it upon yourself to do the work. Churches are like schools, they will guide you to a certain point, but you must do the work . Once you put the work in, then God steps in and takes over. God takes over when you let go. He will begin to manifest in your life, like you never imagined. All you need to do is plant seeds, God will nurture that seed into fruition.

THE SPIRIT OF JEALOUSY

There are many times of spirits. Good spirits and evil spirits.

The spirit of jealousy is an evil and demonic spirit that inhabits in people who are not awake or close to the lord. When someone is jealous of you, it can become dangerous. They become possessive and develop an obsession over s person or thing. The person possessed with the spirit of jealousy, may not even be aware why they act in such a way. The person that is possessed just wants to have, be alike to be in control of everything surrounding the obsessed person. Person who make themselves open to this demonic spirit are those who have the tendency to envy others. They are not typically happy or secure with themselves. It is like a narcissist. When they find someone, who makes them feel better about themselves, they can become possessive for fear of losing this person. Many times, things or relationships are just made up in the person with the spirit of jealousy's imagination.

We are a living prophecy and not even know it. Just as the bible says that sin will consume you and your life, well there are people living in America and around the world, who are so consumed with greed, pride and selfishness, that they do not notice it. Any thoughts of questioning them, is automatically out of the question. What happened to constructive criticism? Now it is considered as hate. We have the blind leading the blind.

Which brings me to the topic of many "so called churches in America. Pastors blindly leading the blind. Many become pastors do they can have a certain lifestyle. These are wolves in sheep's clothing. They are not preaching for the love of God; they are preaching for the love of money. God says if you love me, then feed my sheep.

I believe that the reason many church going Christians do not get sanctified or take it seriously, is became of church offerings. Even though it is great to support the church and help maintain it, church leaders must give more. When I say more, I mean more of the word of God. Pastors need to show passion and truth in their preaching. The word of God is created to stir and make motions. Church goes are more likely to respect their churches and pastors, if they see that the pastor has a backbone.

In the book of second kings' chapter 22 verse 4-7 "Go up to Hilkiah the high priest, that he may count the money which has been brought into the house of the lord, which the door keepers have gathered from the people. And let them deliver it into the hand of those doing the work, who are the over seers in the house of the lord; let them give it to those who are in the house of the lord doing the work, to repair the damages of the house to carpenters and builders and masons- and to buy timber and hewn stones to repair the house. However there need be no accounting made with them of the money delivered into their hand, because they deal faithfully."

Many churches and church leaders take this passage and misuse it to manipulate the congregation. Yes God says to help the church. He also says be a cheerful giver. God says that the money received by the church, should go into the structure of the church. Even though He says that church leaders do-not need to show any record of the money, He is not saying that pastors should go out and buy mansions and lavish cars. Because after all when it is dealt faithfully, they do not need to steal from God. Taking church money is like stealing from God and his ministries. Because the Bible says that we are not to question a pastor regarding church finances, is where they feel the need to misuse and misrepresent the scriptures.

Are pastors supposed to be a representation of God?

Was Jesus Well dressed? Jesus Christ was born in a manger. That was the best way of coming to this world with humility. He could have been born in a palace, and dressed like the king that he is, but that would defeat his purpose.

When a pastor and his wife is living lavishly while the church cannot afford to pay church workers and ministry workers, is the church finances being dealt faithfully? I think not. Nobody minds that their pastors and wives are well taken care of, but when I come to church take care of me. I want the pastor to preach the word of God like it is awfully expensive, like his nice shiny suit.

If the leaders want to be taken care of by God, they better feed his flock.

Because it is embarrassing and a sign of disrespect to our elders, to question or correct them, we remain in the dark.

Just like in the book of kings, many of the kings did evil in the sight of the lord, and this repetition continued for ages because is seen as a taboo or wrong to question authority.

Attending church is not super to be like attending a nightclub. You are charged a fee to sit-in, dance and mingle with others. Pastors should preach every church day like it is the last time, they will get to attend. You will see the goats separate from the sheep quick. It is not the number of heads you can to church, it is the number of souls that you are reaching. Going to some churches are like signing up for a theology class. Everyone is getting-the knowledge, but no-one is receiving the holy ghost.

America is known for being great. Known as the best nation, to be successful. It is known for its best Doctors, lawyers, Universities, and the place to have the best opportunities. So, knowing that, why are we punish for wanting the best? For demanding respect from others? Nothing good comes easy. So why is that fact that if you are a fighter, of your life and those you love, why does that make you a rebel? I mean it is not like success is handed to you. This nation is great because of fighters of the past. People who speak out when they see people doing wrong, it is because they too want to make America greater, but for everyone, not just the rich. Why are Christians see as those who spread hate? Why is it that every non-Christian is automatically come first? If you think about, historical events connect.

Even around the world God's people are persecuted. After slavery was emancipated, came, Jim crow and the civil rights. All along these events, Christians where always persecuted, and so were the blacks, but the difference is that it's on the internet today Thus leading to this day when followers of Christ and the Israelites are severely persecuted. I am talking about the real Israelites that were separated from the God of Israel because of disobedient.

People want what their destiny tells them they should want. For example, if you are a wealthy person, then you are more likely going to look for someone like you? Because if you try and look outside your box, you will end up with insecurities. You will never get what you are looking for. If you are wealthy and are with a person who is not wealthy, you will be stuck wondering if they are with you for what you have. I am not saying that other wealthy people will not try to be with another wealthy person for gains.

If you are a spiritual person, and if you are with a non-spiritual or non-God-fearing person, it is not going to work. The non-spiritual person is going to end being an energy vampire, whose sole purpose is to suck you dry, not to uplift you.

The same as someone bringing with another to help their careers move up. Unless you are incredibly careful and noticeably clear from the beginning of what it is you want and expect, it is not going to work.

In the bible God states clearly states that He made a covenant with Noah, his sons, and all creatures of the earth, that He would never again destroy the earth by a flood. Thus, he says that a rainbow in the clouds, is a reminder of this covenant. Which brings me to homosexuality, which is clearly stated in the bible, as a sin. Now if the lgbtq community disrespects and disobey God commands, why would they turn around and take the rainbow as their symbol. One of the verses of which is found in revelations 22:18-19 kjv it states, "I testify to everyone who hears the words of prophecy of this book: If anyone adds to these things, God will add to him the plagues that are written in this book. And if anyone takes away from the words of the of this prophecy, God shall take away his part from the book of life." As Christians our job is too preach what the word of God says. Or else we would not be true Christians. Non-believers will call you a hater, or bigot, but also call you a fake Christian when you do not act perfect. No one is perfect, not even Christians. Christ is the only perfect being who has walked this earth.

Why is it ok for no believers to judge and persecute followers of Christ, with no punishment like us believers receive when we stand our ground? No matter what religion, group, or people with certain set of beliefs, they do not need to expose your genitals in public and hydrate Themselves in front of children.

If is fine to get your rights in society or communities. No-one is saying they should not have those rights. But some of our rights should be kept in the privacy of our bedrooms. I mean we all know what penises and testicles look like. The straight community is not going out in public and humping each other like dogs. Night clubs are for that purpose.

Despite what anyone teaches their children, whether it be about the lgbtq community or straight community, our children have the rights to remain pure and keep their innocence for as long as possible.

I believe that exposing children to any kind of sexual acts is considered child abuse. How many sex offenders and child predators are registered sex offends we have today? In the words of G. Craig Lewis "pretty soon the sex offenders will be asking for their rights." What happened to the days when we put children first? Now we cannot wait to get them out of the home.

The devil is also after children and their innocence. Many children across the world experience trauma resulting in loss of their innocence as it is. Why are we helping the enemy traumatize and destroy our children? Like I said before, even if you are beliefs are different than mine, I believe you still deserve your rights. Now I might tell you what God's words say, but ultimate God is the true and ultimate judge. Us Christians are just planters of seeds. God is the nurturer, and only he knows what is going to become of you. We are all brothers and sisters. Even though we may not like each other.

When people go to interviews or some professional occasion, they will receive constructive criticism. What do they do with it? Apply themselves and become greater. So, we wonder as Christians why are we hated? Jesus said that "they hated me first." So, it is in fact, the spiritual words of God, that cuts people deep. It is not you or me. It is the "sword" of God.

A lot of people say "do not judge me. Only God can judge me"

What we as believe do is not judgement, but merely correction. We are the messengers. Since Christians are having any to world, we are disrespected, hated ostracized and walked all over like mats. When in fact we have been given the authority by God. Not the authority of this world. Meaning we still need to respect Authority, and at the same time you have a spiritual authority. Spiritual authority which helps you get through life, with wisdom, boldness, and knowledge. I do believe that God wanted some authority in the world and society. Not everyone in this world with chose to be a righteous person, and I believe that for that we need worldly authorities.

When you are led by your flesh, it only leads to sin and death.

Not in the sense to overthrow anyone or anything, but the authority comes from our mouths. Speaking the word and living by God's commandments.

Gods words will do for itself like a double-edged sword.

Like a postal service worker would deliver mail. He did not write or send the mail or create the bills; he is simply a messenger. When the mail worker delivers bills, do we begin to hate him? See true followers and believer of Christ do not hate homosexuals. It is the act of homosexual that God hates. God hates the act of committing homosexual acts, but still loves that person like any other. Even though the Jews were his people, he loves every person.

Which is why he died at the cross, so that we may all be saved through him.

We are commanded by God to love our brother. In John 2:9 "He who says he is in the light, and hates his brother, is in darkness. Until now." Many people say they are Christians but are in-fact deceived. Unfortunately, those people are the ones getting all the recognition. Whenever something is from the devil, it gains a lot of attention and distraction. Distraction from what really matters. Distraction from the word of God and his ways. Unfortunately, the media is very good at creating lies and false claims. We are born into sin and need Christ to deliver us from destruction. The lord is a merciful and loving God, that he will take baby steps for as long as it takes to get you to the finish line. God is the ultimate judge. I would rather be rebuked and corrected, so when I go before the king, I will be ready. I want to hear those words, well done my faithful servant. Not these words saying, "depart from me . I never knew you." One of the things about the word of God, is that it goes straight to the heart and penetrates it. Although Jesus can bring peace to your life, he did not come to the earth to bring peace. He came to the earth so that we may be saved through him. So, Jesus came to deliver us from this world. We may live here physically, but we must not be content to the things of this world. In john 2:15-16 it says, "Do not love the world or things in the world. If anyone loves the world, the love of the father is not in him." "for all that is in the world the lust of the flesh, lust of the eyes and the pride of life is not of the father but is of the world." He tells us not to love things of this world such as materialism, sin, money, fornication, crime etc.

Followers of Christ must be loving but wise. We need to have discernment to know when you are being attacked. The enemy is wiser than us. He knows what buttons to press. What lies to tell. He knows you better than yourself. That is why you must keep the armor of god to protect you from any acts against you. We must also be aware of people in our daily lives. God says "Beloved, do not believe every spirit, but test the spirits, whether they are of God.; because many false prophets have gone out into the world. By this you know the spirit of God; every spirit that confesses that Jesus Christ has come in the flesh of God. And every spirit that does not confess that Jesus Christ has come in the flesh is not of God. And this is the spirit of the antichrist, which you have heard was coming. Is now already in the world." John4:1-3

What God is saying is that those who deny his exist or fail to acknowledge that he is god, means they are of the antichrist spirit. Then on the second epistle of john verse seven it states, "For many deceivers have gone out into the world who do not confess Jesus Christ as coming in the flesh." This is deceiver and an antichrist. Even pastors and preachers who are not preaching the word of god, but instead preach about prosperity and preach heresy are all antichrist.

You do not have to be a horrible person to be antichrist. Just living your life and not giving God any recognition or glory, is of the antichrist.

Living in this day in 2019, many think that it is only an antichrist being that we must watch out for. Do not be deceived. The antichrist Christ spirit is already here. I am talking about spiritual ware fare, not the flesh and blood. The antichrist spirit lingers in world principalities and world leaders, witchcraft and the new age philosophies and belief. Anything that is meant to draw you away from Christ, is dwelling in the spirit of the antichrist. Believe me, the antichrist spirit is very cunning and deceiving. Most people will not even know that they were caught in the antichrist spirit till they are in the middle of troubles they cannot get themselves out of. They will require divine help. Even those who are faithful in the lord Jesus Christ, will find challenges in the last days. As believers we must not faint heart.

For god tells us, "you are of God, little children, and have overcome them, because he who is in you is greater than he who is in the world." Plus, God will never leave nor forsake us. But we must do our part. We are the ones who walk away from God, not him leaving us. John4:4 so never lose hope, god is always with us, even when it does not feel like it.

During the end times the bible says that things will be revealed unto us. We will have revelations on top of revelations. In the end times, which is the present times, many will see those who are for you as opposed to ghost who say they are for you. They say that as you get older, your friends circle gets smaller. As a believer of Christ, your circle will get even smaller. Family will turn against family. The good things will be considered bad. And the bad things will be considered good. As days go by, it will be more of a challenge for all. Meaning that as time draws near, the spirit of antichrist will have complete control over unbelievers. There are too many deceiving spirits that can be difficult for some to recognize. To not know God, is to be dead. Those who are dead in the spirit will not be able to resist antichrist spirits, nevertheless the real beast of revelations.

People who are problematic are always looking for problems. Not to solve them, but to relish in the drama and to see what they can take from others. They need to line of supply. I mean, many are like vampires, are only in others' lives as a parasite. For example, a dude with a few baby mommas, will come in your life to cause more problems. In the meantime, trying to make you look like you are the problem when you were living your life. You might have one child, but this person makes you out to look like some whore. Really? When he is the one with two or three baby mommas? I am not saying that all baby mommas are problematic. I am a single mother. And I am always going to stick up for other sisters, of course if they are in their right mind, because I know the struggles that single mothers face every day. The struggles they face because of society marginalizing them. Because instead of men realize that women, especially single mothers are treated poorly in society. Without women, society wall cave. Many programs that is "supposed" created for women are nothing more than society's Affirmative action. We do not want to be labeled as a sexist society, so therefore we will create just enough, to keep women in their place. We will not create more than enough programs, to ensure that women get the equal opportunities that men do.

Society wants to use God's commands to remind us of our places. But do you remember what commands that God has for you? As a society, as a leader, as a man? Before people tell others where they belong, tell them to clean the specks on their eyes first.

What everyone seems to forget, is that Christians are not perfect. The do not know that Christians are at war 24/7. It does not end for us; from the time we wake up in the morning till bedtime. Christians are always on their guard, because when you are trying to live a holy life, that is when the enemy attacks your life. So, we should not put all Christians in the same box. God says know them by their fruits. So, you need to try everyone who says that they are Christians. Even though they might be quoting scriptures, but if their character does not match up, he or she is a liar.

Another thing I would like to address, is that a true child of God is more likely to face struggles. It may seem the opposite, but it is not. When you think about it. If you say you are a Christian but living in sin, but your life seems to be in order from the outside. You can have all the money in the world, a nice home, a nice car, and a family. But inside you can be so miserable. You can be incomplete even though you are married. You have everything of this world, so you feel there is no need to pray. That is the mistakes of many Christians out there. Once they get to a point where they have all they dreamed of, they begin to distance themselves from God. That is an extremely dangerous thing to do. It is dangerous because you are giving the enemy more room inn-your life to cause you to sin. When the enemy deceives you, you will not even see it coming.

The problem with a-lot of Christians, is that they believe that when the blessings from God come, that no struggles can come. That is how we fall.

We receive like we are entitled and well deserved, that when we get what we deserve, we break down. We blame God. We stop going to church. We stop praying. We get into our child tamper mode. We become de pleated.

And then we must go back down that path to regain our place in God's word. But the next time around you will be stronger and wise. But you will develop humility, discipline, and obedience. Once you achieve those three things, then you really begin to get to God who god really is. You get to feel who God is. Rather than just reading about him, you will get to experience him.

You will get to experience God in different ways.
Everyone has a gift from God, in his ministries.
Whether it is feeling other people's emotions so deep. So that you can be used by God to help heal others.
Whether it is the gift of prophesying or laying hands on people for prayer and healing.

Or you could be called to travel and preach the gospel.

One of the reasons God has not came back, is because he is waiting till his message is preached on all corners of the earth. He gave his son, so who ever believes in him shall not parish but have ever last life. How can people say that God does not care? He is the essence of patience. So instead of acting ungrateful because you want him to come because of your problems, he is thinking about all souls.

We need to learn how to worship and give God the glory even when you are struggling. Even when we are sick and going through tough times.

I admit even I struggle at times and become frustrated at life. That is because I am trying to do things God does not want me to do. I am probably trying to do what is not meant for me.

We cannot let the world's voices keep us from hearing a God's voice.

The importance of spending time alone.

We are all spiritual beings. We all are carrying around different spirits. Some godly spirits and some demonic spirits. So, when you interact with others on a daily level, especially for those who work jobs. You will meet many types of spirits. You need to be wearing your armor of God. See even though you are not going to bed with everyone you meet, being in the presence of something who could possibly have many demonic spirits attack to them, could put you at risk for influence. You can be affected by evil spirits. I am not saying to do not that you should never get in contact with others, because you might be the one that God uses to help deliver someone from demonic possession.

Getting demonic possession is like having STDS of the spirit. You got to remember Christians are dealing with twice as many struggles as a normal random person. It may not be physically or financially, but spiritually. That is why spiritual tend to be or appear as being weird from the rest of society. Not that we are trying to prove a point, but when we discover how to be more spiritual, we are less fleshy. I done expect those who do not know what I am talking about to understand. It is an experiencing rather than knowing.

Taking time for yourselves, is important because, you need to remind yourself who you are and that you are on a mission. God needs you to be focused, and not get caught up with society and with others, who do not have the same vision as you. Real Christians need to constantly feed themselves with the word of God. We are like empaths, who go out in the world full and come back home deflated. There for we have got to building ourselves up repeatedly.

THE LOVE OF SIN

I used to love sin

I loved sin when I was living in sin. Now that I have a relationship with God, I hate sin. All though I do hate sin, I still love the sinners, for I was lost, and God did not desert me like I deserved.

The love of sin is one of the reasons people refuse the gospel and find living a holy life boring. When I first began my journey as a newly reborn Christian, I was in it just because I feared going to hell. I did know or care about how God could change me as a person. I was worried about not being able you go out every weekend with friends. But it when you let God enter your heart, you no-longer have the desires to sin. Sin does not seem like sin to sinners.

Sinning In today's communities, is seen as the norm. Society no longer live Godly lives due to generations of parenting without having God in their lives. As time changes, so do laws in our societies that make it difficult for others to openly worship God.

Back to my topic of sinning. When a person does not know what a good and healthy thing is, how will they know what something good is. God is bad according to some people, who are only used to sinning or an arrogant heart.

TESTING SPIRITS

A lot of people profess to be this and that, but when it comes down to prove it, they are full of excuses. That is why is why God says to test their spirits. If someone says that whey is born again Christians, but are continually sinning with no repentance, he is a Liar! God also says of anyone who is a liar, is of your father, Satan. It is too easy to say that people who have power and wealth are evil. Most people are not bad people from the beginning. Throughout the process of gaining wealth, status, and power, they forget where they come from. Some forget their humble beginnings. As they accumulate status, they become self-righteous and exalt themselves. In the book of Hosea, God's word says how Israel has rebelled against him. In Hosea chapter 7:1-4 "when I would have healed Israel, then the iniquity of Ephraim was uncovered, and wickedness of Samaria. For they have committed fraud; A thief comes in. A band of robbers take spoil outside. They do not consider in their hearts that I remember all their wickedness; now their own deeds have surrounded the; They are before my face. They make a king glad about their wickedness, and princes with their lies."

This just proves that the world and many industries are driven by the worship of Satan. As the bible states that Lucifer exalted himself, instead of being humble and giving glory to god, which was the reason for his creation. Lucifer was the most beautiful angel of God. But when he got cast down from heaven, he was no longer an angel of God. Along with Lucifer went some of the other angels who followed Lucifer to rebellion and damnation . In Hosea chapter 7:7 it also states "They are all hot, like an oven, and have devoured their judges; all their kings have fallen. No one among them calls upon me." Everyone who ever thought that they could become better than the lord of heavens, have failed.

Many organizations and churches today, also place church members on a platform, who do not even belong up there. Therefore, leading God's sheep to iniquity. In Hosea chapter 8 verse 4 it states "They set up kings, but not by me; They made princes, but I did not acknowledge them. From their silver and gold, they made idols for themselves. That they might be cut off."

We cannot continue to raise and exalt people who are not sanctified or called by the lord. See when we do things in the lord's name, it should be out of the pureness of our hearts. We cannot not delude or defile what is supposed to be holy. We as people need to be humble in the presence of God and as we minister to others, but also raise our standards and realize that we deserve so much better as a God's people. He wants us to live clean lives, not to punish us but because he loves us. We listen to society and the world, more than we do God. Many of us do-not do it out of spite, but because we live in a fast-paced world. We are so busy with everything else, but we find it difficult to give God a little bit of our time. We are missing the most important part of our lives if we cannot put time aside to acknowledge and spend time with him. The issue is that we have too many things going on in our lives. To many unimportant and useless things, that take a-lot of our time.

Things like idols. We worship things in our lives, that may not even see like it. For example, money, job, materials, celebrities etc. if there is something in your life taking much of your time, instead of God, then you may be worshiping idols. It does not have to be a person or deity. Hosea chapter 12:4-6 "yet I am the lord your God, ever since the land of Egypt, and you shall know no God but Me. For there is no savior besides me. I knew you in the wilderness, in the land of great drought. When they gad pasture, they were filled; they were filled, and their heart was exalted. Therefore they forgot me."

THE SPIRIT OF STAGNATION

We are all unique and have our own destiny. Our separate paths, ideas separate desires that God puts inside each one of us. Some people discover it and some never do. I believe to know what your call or destiny is, you must know that God is god. You must know it and want it. What you can never do, is allow anyone to overshadow your desires in life with their desires. Who knows God may have a plan for you that cannot be overshadowed?

Churches these days act like they are too righteous to welcome people. Churches are becoming more like state institutions, which they were separated from, all these rules and regulations, that they forget that they ate there for Christ. The church is supposed to uplift the body of Christ. And the individuals going to church, are the church.

Many people think that Christians or followers of Christ are supposed to be people pleasers. That is further from the truth. At least not true believers. The moment you give your life to God, you are to give up pleasing yourself. You are to give up pleasing the world. As a believer of Christ your responsibility as a Christian, is to put God first and be obedient. The bible says you cannot worship both God and mammal. You cannot worship more than one god, because you will hate one and love the other.

People deal with institutionalized organizations every day. No one wants to go to church and must take a ticket like at the department of motor vehicles. Churches want to act like the world when they are called to be separate.

Churches are giving positions to any person, claiming they are righteous. They give positions out more than employment managers. Then wonder why the congregation begin placing these church leaders in higher place.

Right has nothing to do with religion.

I also wanted to address my opinions and beliefs on the topic of homosexuality. I want to discuss the fact that our rights as Americans has nothing to do with our children, who will grow up to make their own decisions. Just like God gave us free will to choose after He has warned Adam and Eve. Therefore, we teach our children and warn them about things of life. When they are old enough to decide, they will choose which way they want to go. What we can and should is stop bullying. Bullying is one of the key factors, that fuel this movement, making others who have different beliefs looking like hateful bigots. Everyone agrees that we should look out for the children. But when it comes to the LGBTer movement, they want to shove it down our kid's throat. We might as we change consent age, buy our children boxes of cigarettes, and send them to the liquor store. Children's minds are fragile and susceptible to influence. Children agree with adults because they think it will make them happy. I believe that even a psychologist, would find this disturbing.

Which brings me to the same sex public bathrooms. I do not agree with it. Even those who agree with that, would not like it if someone older adult went in the bathroom after their own child. They would probably kill that person. When it comes to your children, I do not blame some people who go through extreme measures for their children's sake.

When it comes to satisfaction, nobody is good at it.

Meaning there is no human being that will total satisfy your every need. The only person who can satisfy your every need is God. God is the only one who knows our desires and wants. A sincere relationship with God will leave you feeling complete.

As humans we tend to expect too much from others, which can leave us feeling disappointed when they fail to satisfy our every need.

People in Christian must deal with things and situations differently because people expect much more from "spirituality people." As if that gives others who are of the world, an excuse to not try very hard.

People expect so much from Christians like they have superpowers. It is only God that can expect that much from you, to push you so you will not break.

Human beings like you push others to the point that they may break.

Which is why it is important to know your limits, and to tell others your limit.

For example, people who are still of the world will look for every reason why you are not living your best potential but will never provide a solution to that problem.

So when you become a child of God, you got have boundaries and reinforce them. If not, people will walk all over you till you become drained.

Do not expect a non-believer to understand you. When you decide to stop living a sinful life, that's when sin comes knocking at your door.

The devil knows more than we give him credit for. He will try every and use everyone in your life you try and deceive you.

See when you become a child of God, your whole thinking process changes.

You become more progressive in everything you do.

You become less tolerable of nonsense.

Everyone else will begin to think that you are acting like a snob.

You don' desire to be bothered by pettiness.

You either value or devalue everything. Even though it might not seem like it to the world, you live for a purpose.

So do not feel like you have got to lower yourself self-respect to fit in with the world.

When you become a child of God, it could take years of progression to become full secure as a child of God. Beware of stans devices. Satan is always looking for whom he may devoir. People go through life and come to the lord at an older age and wonder why you are so self-righteous.

It is like, you took the time, sacrificed years of your life to getting to know God. Here comes someone, who feels like you should move heaven and earth for them? Excuse me?

If I am the one trying to get right with God, why are you the one feeling like you are so worthy.

God says help others without expecting in return, because in helping others, in a way its serving God. But people tend to take advantage of this. They want the blessing of God, while being unworthy.

I mean they will try to ruin your relationship with God. I am not insinuating that we are all deserve God's mercy. But Christ still gave His life for all.

Everyone has their own cross to carry.

A lot of people want you to carry your cross and their cross.

It doesn't work that way.

That is why it's called a relationship with God'

Not a "take advantage of someone relationship"

DEPRESSION

The number of Americans with depression is staggering. Especially among those who face traumatic situations and struggles.

Everyone is prone to depression, but are Christians supposed to be depressed? Not to say they will not, but from a biblical point of view.

Christians deal with attacks from the devil day and night, so they must always have their guards up.

Which is a taboo in society. Society is telling you to let your guard down so you can make friends. Usually ending up meeting unwanted friends. There are all kinds of people in this world with all kinds of energy and spirituality, you got to always protect yourself spirituality.

What many Christians tend to fall under, is situations that cause them to have melancholy, and can bounce back as soon as they remain that they are a child of God.

However those of those of the world do not always have the same opportunity. For instance those suffering from addiction, abuse, death of loved ones, or other traumas. Although we have resources to help those suffering from depression, it is not the healing that they can get from God.

Many Americans are depressed because they take pills to cope with every problem they have. There is s pill or a quick solution for everything. But the one that really matters, which is the soul, is not healed.

Everything someone feels today

It is not tolerable. We have tons of religions but non heal the soul, like Christ

We live in a non-spiritual world, a lot of Americans are dead inside, because of the cultures in America that satisfies instant gratification and does not truly heal deep emotions and do not solve real problems. Everything is swept under the rug. We put Band-Aids on all windows and do not properly heal those wounds.

One misconception that the world believes, is that Christ came to cause peace. When he comes again, he is not coming to make peace. He is coming for division of goof s as and evil. The first time He died was for salvation. When he returns, you better be ready. The time to get right with God is right now, not when it is too late. I am glad and thankful that I did not die before I had the chance to get to know Christ. Once you are physically dead, there is no going back.

You know a-lot of religions promise peace, but Christ promises salvation. That salvation will get you the peace your soul needs. Christ is the water that will quench your thirst and you will never thirst again. He is the bread of life.

Another way I look at it is, Christ is here to satisfy every void in a person being. You know some people meet others whom they say is their soulmates and others never get that experience in life. Well Christ is that soulmate for all. I know it sounds like a cliché, but it is true.

Many people think that Christianity is just reading the bible, going to church, and doing good deeds.

There is more to it. Anyone can read the bible. It takes a relationship with God to be a Christian. Knowing him and being Christ like.

When others have not healed from their sinful past

As a child of God, you go through a lot emotionally and spiritually.

People raise their expectations of you, but in secret.

They want to tell you what is right and what is not right, while making excuses for them making bad choices.

They want it to be ok to accept poor judgement from them, but still be your best.

They are not ashamed to accept or take from you but not give you the pedestal you deserve.

When you come to Christ, you become a different creature. Not physically but mentally and spiritually.

Christians are not perfect and will on occasions fall for temptation but are not bad people because of it. Christians are attacked the most out of others day and night.

Because they are tempted day and night it is easy for others to who do not understand what it really is to be a Christian, to thin bad of them.

Boldness is not arrogance

As Christians the bible tells us to be meek, gentle, kind, and loving.

That is what everyone seems to think anyways. But people forget to mention the other sides of how a Christian should be. Christ is symbolized as a lamb because he is so gentle and pure. He is also symbolized as a lion, for he is bold and strong. He is also symbolized as a dove, which also signifies purity.

So it is okay for Christians to get bent out of shape at times, if it is for corrections leading to the will of God.

A lot of times people do-not want to let go of the "old You" therefore putting you in a compromising situation.

We got to deal with people in accordance to God's words. At times people will get upset because the word of God is contradicting over their sinful ways.

But they believe that it is you, the Christian who is offensive.

Although we should choose our words what we say to people, we do not always do that. Many times it is because we say things out of emotions.

It is alright to have thoughts but choose our words carefully. As humans, that is not what we do. That is why God does not punish us for our thoughts. It is the action follows a thought that will get us into problems.

If God punished us for our thoughts, we would be extinct as human beings. Satan is constantly trying to mislead us by putting evil thoughts in our minds.

Satan bothers those that are not his children.

That is why it is so easy to say, "they are not Christians, but they have everything they want in life."

Or do they? They have what they want and think they want. Satan does not bother those who are doing his work but will drop you off the face of this planet without a thought.

When are people going to realize that just because you are not in any immediate danger, that it is all good?

It is like belong to a gang or mob. If you are doing what the boss pleases, you get to keep your life. God lets things like this exist in our lives, as warning of what is to come if we continued to live a sinful life.

Like with diseases and illness that we face in this world, are warnings that it could get worse if we do-not rectify our lives.

We all have our moments where we want to pout and throw tantrums like children, when we down want to obey God's commands or when we face struggles.

That is why we are known as children of God. There is not surpassing Him. We will never be greater, so there is no point in trying. No need to act like you are more righteous than God.

When you face situations where people want to use your faith against you, to excuse the fact that they are not mentally and spiritually at your level. It is okay to stand up for yourselves as bold children of God.

To others who are spiritually blind, and not able to see the reason for your purpose.

I have put a-lot of work into becoming what I am today, not to sound arrogant or anything like it.

You cannot tell me that you want to join me but expect me to go down to the lower levels.
If I came to you wanting to join you, that is another story.
I say this because there are people in life, that want to reap but are not willing to do the sewing.

You cannot wing your way into heaven. You cannot ride on another person's salvation. Pick up your own cross.

THINGS CAN CARRY SPIRITS

Most of us know that God says to do not make any image of him nor worship idols. When God says not to take any image or create idols, he is saying it for a purpose. Ever heard "Everything has a spirit." That is true. Example you buy a garden statue at a yard sale. The person who was the previous owner may have been into demonic stuff. They may have used the statues for ritual purposes or any ungodly thing. Prayer is important, especially over things that you put in your homes. You got to be careful not to bring any demonic force inside your home if you are a child of God. An example is, let us say your faith is like an infant. Meaning you are clean and pure. Upon taking the infant-outside the house, it risks being exposed to bacteria and harmful objects. Your relationship with God is precious and must be cared for.

People say that the fool always thinks he is right. That a fool will not listen to anyone but their own understanding.

I-say that we as Christians should not lean on our own understandings and trust in God because he knows what he is doing. Nor should a Christian lean on the understanding of others, especially if they do not profess to be a Christian. Christians already must have discernment because there are many wolves in sheep clothing.

Many people misquote this scripture. They take it and base it on themselves when giving advice. God did not say lean on the understandings of your friends and people who call themselves Christians.

See although being a believer in Christ, means to sacrifice the self. Meaning that you shift your focus on yourself and turn that focus on God.

The only time it should be okay to be selfish, is if you ate spending your time on the word of God. You can be selfish in learning about God's ways for yourself. For your salvation.

The rest of the time, you should be concerned with the service to God. The service to humanity and Hid flock. But be diligent and discerning of the wolves in sheep clothing.

Some people will have the angle persona and not do anything angelic for others.

They will have that arc angel look, with the flowy hair, looking like super models.

God sends angels for a purpose, to help others, not to pose in front of you, expecting you to give to them. There is nothing wrong with giving, but in this case, we are talking about angelic personas.

I do not mean to sound funny, but it is true.

It is like they have an entitled beggar attitude.

The both lines are, if all you do is take from people, God is going to take from you. If you give others willingly, God will give to you. Give with no resentment.

It seems that we are in a generation where every time we make mistakes, and sin, who go out and create a community. If we fall short, we will go out and form a falling short community. It sounds petty. The devil is petty.

I am not looking down on support groups that support good causes, but I think we need to draw a line. Instead of healing passed through these traumas, we go and put a bowtie on it. We spray the filth with fragrance and continue.

Placing idols before God

In the book Colossians chapter two verse 21-23, God is talking about being aware of the deceitfulness of false teachings. Its states "Do not touch, do not taste, do not handle, which all concerns these things which perish with the using. According to the commandments and doctrines of men? These things indeed have an appearance of wisdom in self-imposed religion, false humility, and neglect of the body, but are of no value against the indulgence of the flesh." (kjv)

The lord is not about doing favors for people. He is about saving souls. Do not think that Jesus is your special genie, that you can pray only when you need something. When you finally decide to take God seriously, he will answer your questions and give you the desires of your heart. When I started my relationship with God, I met someone at the wrong timing. But he felt so right. I was put in a position where I had to prove that my heart for God was more important than this person. It hurt like hell, but it was not meant to be. I thought I would never move past that, but I did. If I had stay in contact with this person, I would have never gotten this close to God.

Sometimes God must let your heart break before he can start building you up. Now that I am older, I realize that a lot of things we want as young people, are not always best for us. I began liking this person so much, that back then probably would have put him before God. He saw that and removed me from the situation. I would question why he would take away someone I cared so deep for, but not being mature enough or rational to realize why he did it. Like a parent spoiling a child's fun to protect them. When you are young, you are so dramatic about everything. So that is one of the reasons why the lord is not quick to anger and has patience with us. Many people growing physically, but mentally they are like fools. Wisdom does not come with age. The bible says the fear of God is the beginning of wisdom. When you grow, you must put away all childish things.

Also, when you give your life to God, you must be reborn in Christ.

In Colossians chapter three verse 5-6(kjv)It states "therefore put to death your members which are on earth, fornication, uncleanliness, passion, evil desire, and covetousness, which is idolatry. Because these things the wrath of God is coming upon the sons of disobedience, in which you yourselves once walked when you lived in them.

I was new to the word of God and not strong at all. From the foolishness and uncleanliness. Although we may fall occasionally, God is merciful to forgive us, because he loves us.

Therefore, when you become a child of God, you must put away all your earthly titles. Every single person in Christ is to put away their old ways and follow Christ.

In the end times people will turn away from the word of God. Even some Christians will turn away. From their faith. The good will be considered bad, and what is bad will be considered good. Family will turn against each other. There will be so much disorder and iniquities in the world, that those who do not know or hear the truth will indulge in their sinful nature. The righteous things will be unrighteousness. In the book of first Timothy chapter four verses 1-3(kjv) "Now the spirit expressly says that in latter times some will depart from the faith, giving heed to deceiving spirits and doctrines of demons, speaking lies in hypocrisy, having their own conscience seared with a hot iron, forbidding to marry and commanding to abstain from foods which God created to be received with thanksgiving by those who believe and know the truth."

And also Second Timothy chapter three verses 1-5 "know this, that in the last days perilous times will come: For men will be lovers of themselves, lovers of money, boasters, proud, blasphemers, disobedient to parents, unthankful, unholy, unloving, unforgiving, slanderers, without self-control, brutal, despisers of good, traitors, headstrong, haughty, lovers of pleasure rather than lovers of God, having a form of godliness but denying it's power. And from such people turn away!"

PARENTING

It is said in the bible, that parents have so much influence on their child's and grandchildren's children. Meaning that how parents decide to live their life, will affect their off springs and future generations. If you obey God and lead a holy life, you will find favor with God. And therefore, blessing your family and future generations. Like Abraham, who was obedient towards God, was blessed by God. Abraham's blessings came in having many nations after him. God's favor towards Abraham follows till this day in 2019, through Jesus Christ.

Many of us are born into dysfunctional families, with no leadership, no love, no obedience because most people do not worship the Lord Jesus Christ, either because do not know him, worship false Gods or never gave him a chance. Now we cannot pick what families we are born into. The sins of our parents or ancestors will catch up to future off springs if not repented. If their sins are not repented, curses may be form against the future generations. In Zechariah chapter the bible speaks of the holy city and God's people. The book of Zechariah states "For thus says the Lord of hosts; Just as I determined to punish you when your fathers provoked Me to Wrath, says the Lord of hosts, And I would not relent, So again in these days I am determined to do good to Jerusalem and to the house of Judah." (9:14-15kjv.) so God gives us chances to break the curse and cycles in our lives. To break generational curses we must live an obedient life, believe that Christ died for our sins to be set free from sin. Which is why the bible says we are born in sin. We must be born again in Christ.

What you worship, will affect your children, whether they decide to go their own way. Everything is spiritual. When a woman is with child, that child is receiving everything that the mother is consuming. If she is consuming demonic spirits, the unborn child will also be affected. Even the father's seed, before it is formed into a child, is carrying whatever that man is carrying spiritually.

Before Jesus Christ died for our sins, God's people were saved through the law. After the Exodus of Egypt, God's people were still carrying sin, worshiping false gods which lead to many years of loss and confusion. God sent Jesus Christ, because he knows that although his people was free from pharaoh, spiritually they were defiled. The holy spirit clears you of all in purity and guides the children of God into leading a holy life.

Therefore it is important to first be in the spirit of God, repent of ungodly thoughts, and keep in the word of God as well as in prayer.

The bible says to raise your children in the way they should be, and they will not depart from it.

Although we have the world against us, which makes it difficult to raise our children the way God would want you to. It is difficult when we must obey the government and raise your children the way you want to. Satan always has a plan. Using government institutions, to influence your children is one way the devil can get away with it. You have got the public education system, doing more than teaching your children. Also indoctrinating them with antichrist doctrines. Things that are not biblical, are being forced down our children's minds. Separating the church from state, discreetly stripping Christians rights. Everyone must tolerate every-agenda, but the Christian faith is suppressed. If we are all equal, shouldn't Christians especially parents be able to decide how they want their children raised?

I believe that the Lord God allows his people to live in and go through situations, is do that we may learn endurance, obedience, humbleness and to learn how to love others.

We should obey authorities, because in heaven, we will also have authority.

No one is perfect, there will be people in authority who are not equipped for such leadership roles. Some leaders allow themselves to be used be the devil, leading only by the flesh and not really leading by the authority of the higher power. See many in leadership roles are consumed by themselves. They use their own understandings, rather than to seek God's wisdom. Not leading by God's wisdom, is deadly.

This life is a preparation and training for the next life. That is why we have parents, the Authorities, and annoying neighbors. Another reason why we ho through hard times, is because God is concerned with our souls, not our bodies or materialistic things. I am not saying that God does not care what happens to us, but hid focus id our souls .

The bible says that it is easier for a poor man to get into heaven than a rich man.

The poor are closer to God because they have nothing. I mean, that the little materials that they have, will leave more room for them to look above. The poor are forced to look onto God because of the unlimited time, and the release of the materials that would normally take that time with God. The reason it is difficult for the rich to go to heaven is because they are not consumed by materialism, that they cannot focus on the spiritual. They focus on money and monetary gains. I am not saying all rich people will not go to heaven. Km implying that it is more difficult to gain the kingdom of heaven when your life is the focus of the material world.

The world is ruled by Satan. He is glad when your focus is on the material world.

Unless we pass the test of life, we will not inherit the kingdom of God.

Society tells us what to do, when to do it, how to do it, and in the process tell you how old you are getting.

The enemy is always copying God's creations with counterfeits. The enemy also has a planning for children of God. If you are not honoring him, he will send people to take you down. See the enemy cannot be everywhere like God. That is why he needs his angels too. See if you have God's anointing and protection, the devil cannot get to You himself. He is going to send his demons to go after you and attack your life. Therefore if you are guarded by the armor of God, you will be able to resist him.

The devil is a snake for a reason. He is very conniving.

The biggest lie the devil ever told was, convincing the world that he does not exist.

That is where many of us fall short. The bible is great that if you identify as a follower of Christ, you will not only be labeled crazy, but you will look crazy. That just shows that society has been living backwards-the whole time. Unless you are a diagnosed maniac with violent tendencies. Or if you are possessed by demons.